A TASTE OF CHICKEN SOUP

FOR THE

CHRISTIAN WOMAN'S SOUL

A TASTE OF
CHICKEN SOUP

FOR THE

CHRISTIAN
WOMAN'S SOUL

Stories to Open the Heart and
Rekindle the Spirit

Jack Canfield
Mark Victor Hansen
Patty Aubery
Nancy Mitchell Autio
LeAnn Thieman

Health Communications, Inc.
Deerfield Beach, Florida

www.hcibooks.com
www.chickensoup.com

Bringing It to Pass, Football and All. Reprinted by permission of Patricia Lorenz. ©1995 Patricia Lorenz

The Plan. Reprinted by permission of LeAnn Thieman. ©2001 LeAnn Thieman.

Love Bugs. Reprinted by permission of Darlene Lawson. ©2001 Darlene Lawson.

A Small Unsteady Light. Reprinted by permission of Walker Meade. ©2001 Walker Meade.

Meeting God at 30,000 Feet. Reprinted by permission of Caron Loveless. ©1998 Caron Loveless.

Tammy and the Diamond Dress. Reprinted by permission of Robin Lee Shope. ©1998 Robin Lee Shope.

Ivy's Cookies. Reprinted by permission of Candy Abbott. ©1998 Candy Abbott.

Leadership Material. Reprinted by permission of Nancy Ellen Hird. © 2001Nancy Ellen Hird.

And the Little Child Shall Lead Them. Reprinted by permission of Dawn Nowakoski. ©2000 Dawn Nowakoski.

The Miracle of Medjugorje. Reprinted by permission of LeAnn Thieman. ©2001 LeAnn Thieman.

Do You Believe in God? Reprinted by permission of Lynn Dean. ©1999 Lynn Dean.

Sunset in the Rearview Mirror. Reprinted by permission of Sheryl A. Simons. ©2001 Sheryl A. Simons.

Library of Congress Cataloging-in-Publication Data

© 2006 Jack Canfield and Mark Victor Hansen
ISBN 0-75730-512-1

HCI, its Logos and Marks are trademarks of Health Communications, Inc. Publisher, Health Communications Inc., 3201 SW 15th Street, Deerfield Beach, Fl 33442

We dedicate this book to our mothers who not only formed our lives, but our faiths:

Ellen Taylor

Una Peterson Hansen

Linda Mitchell

Berniece Duello

Contents

Introduction

Since the beginning of time and through-out biblical history, women have inspired and upheld one another by sharing their stories. Sarah's desire for a child reinforces our own, and we find hope and promise in her story. We learn about the thrilling joys and devastating sorrows of motherhood from Mary, the mother of Jesus, who taught us the ultimate lessons in letting go.

During some phases of our lives, we draw strength from Ruth, who selflessly took in her mother-in-law. As we allow others to care for us, we find peace and strength in Naomi. Like Miriam, we dance, sing and rejoice after triumphantly surviving life's difficult journeys. When we step out in new adventures, feeling eager yet confused, we relate to lessons from Eve. Tales of Mary Magdalene remind us to forgive ourselves as Jesus forgives us. And how often have we wished for the wisdom and discernment of the prophetess Deborah?

In compiling the original edition of

Chicken Soup for the Christian Woman's Soul, we read how faith in Christ has blessed women's lives. We hope the stories excerpted here will inspire you to make Him the center of your life. We believe you will draw strength from your fellow sisters in Christ as you practice these lessons of faith, love and forgiveness.

Bringing It to Pass,
Football and All

If you believe, you will receive whatever you ask for in prayer.

MATTHEW 21:22

It was a crisp fall day in Madison, Wisconsin, when our University of Wisconsin football team defeated the University of Illinois in the final Big Ten Conference home game of the season. Now Wisconsin was headed to the Hall of Fame Bowl in Tampa, Florida, over the Christmas holidays. My twenty-two-year-old son, Michael, a senior at University of Wisconsin at Madison, was a four-year member of their marching band, famous for their wildly entertaining high-stepping antics that dazzled crowds.

I'd desperately wanted to go to the Rose Bowl game the year before to watch him perform, but the trip was too expensive. I didn't know anyone in Pasadena to stay with, and airfare was out of the question. On New Year's Day 1994, my house was full of relatives as we all watched Michael on TV. He played his drums with such precision during the Rose Bowl parade and game that my heart nearly burst with excitement and pride.

When the Wisconsin Badgers won the right to play in the Hall of Fame Bowl the very next season, I realized that that game would be Michael's last time ever to march with the band before he graduated. I had to be there. Right!—a single parent with a small income and bigger-than-life dreams; that's me.

In late November I mentioned my dream to my airline pilot friends who use the extra bedrooms in our home as their Milwaukee-area home away from home. One said he had a couple of low-cost "friend" passes that my fifteen-year-old son Andrew and I could use to get to Tampa and back.

"The passes are only about ninety dollars each, round-trip," he said. "But you'll have to fly standby."

I jumped at the chance as he set things in motion. Next, I had to find housing. I looked on the map and saw that our retired friends, Wally and Shirley, lived just forty-five minutes from Tampa. I was sure they'd put us up for the week in their Florida condo.

Everything seemed to be working smoothly until I called my dad in Illinois to tell him the good news. Dad planted my feet back on the ground when he said, "You're going to Florida between Christmas and New Year's? That's the busiest tourist week of the year down there! And you're flying standby? What do you think your chances are of getting on a plane that week?"

My bubble of optimism burst again when I heard on the radio that nearly thirty thousand Wisconsinites had already bought tickets to the Hall of Fame Bowl. Our chances of getting down there flying standby certainly didn't look good. In fact, they looked impossible.

Besides, there was another glitch in the plans. The airline we'd be flying on had only one flight a day to Tampa. How could I even think there'd be empty seats on that plane during the week between Christmas and New Year's?

I told myself disgustedly, *How could you be so stupid? This will never work!*

In addition to decorating for Christmas, buying gifts, cleaning house and planning meals for the holidays, I now had an additional stressor in my life.

I commiserated with my friend Heather, who told me, "Pat, stop worrying. Do something for me. Look through the book of Psalms. Read it until you find a verse that seems to be speaking to you."

"Psalms? What am I going to find in there?" I asked Heather.

"Just do it. You'll find what you're looking for."

That afternoon I opened my Bible and read the first two psalms. Nothing hit me. The third verse said something about a tree yielding "its fruit in season," which only depressed me more. It made me think of ruby-red grapefruit and large, juicy oranges hanging on trees all over Florida—fruit that I certainly wouldn't be enjoying.

This can't be the verse that's supposed to make me feel better, I thought. I closed the book and opened it again at random. This time my eyes went directly to Psalms 37:5: "Commit thy way unto the Lord; trust also in Him; and He shall bring it to pass."

Two things about that verse threw me for a loop. The part about committing my way to the Lord—my way to see my son perform in his last game, perhaps? The other was the notion that the Lord would "do this." If I did my part, then God would do His. In other words, if I really, truly trusted in the Lord, then He would bring all things to pass. That was the clincher, since Andrew and I would be flying standby on a "pass."

I thought, *Okay, Patricia, this is it. If Heather can be so dead-bolt certain of her faith, why can't you? You have to put it on the line. Do you truly believe that this is in the hands of the Lord and that He will bring it to pass?*

I only had to ask myself that question once. I sat down that moment and memorized verse 37:5. It was the first Bible verse I'd ever memorized in my life. I've been a longtime Bible reader and student, but memorizing is very difficult for me. I chanted the verse at least a hundred times a day during those weeks before Christmas: "Commit thy way unto the Lord; trust also in Him; and He shall bring it to pass."

The minute I turned the problem over to the Lord, I relaxed completely and virtually sailed through the preparations for Christmas.

Never again did I worry about whether or not we'd get on the plane, not even when I learned every flight had been greatly over-sold with the exception of Christmas morning. And even for that flight, eighty of the eighty-four seats had been sold, with three weeks still to go before Christmas.

For the next three weeks, I repeated my newly memorized verse a thousand times: before I got out of bed in the morning, before each meal, during the day, in the car, in my home office, walking down the hall, in bed at night. I repeated it to all my friends and family and assured them that Andrew and I would be in Tampa for the Hall of Fame Bowl on January 2, and that we'd be flying down there on Christmas morning.

Christmas Eve day dawned holy and cold in Milwaukee. Andrew, my grown children, son-in-law, granddaughter, and friends Rusty and Heather and their two little daughters, all celebrated Christ's birth amidst my giggling excitement as I packed our bags for Florida. I shared my memorized Bible verse from Psalms with them as part of the grace before our Christmas Eve dinner.

"So Mom, are you just going to keep going back to the airport every day all week until you get on a plane?" my daughter Julia asked during dessert.

"No, honey, we'll be getting on the plane tomorrow morning. I'll send you postcards and bring you seashells!"

Never before in my life had I been so sure of something—something that to all the sensible people around me seemed to be the folly of the century.

Bags packed, car loaded, Michael drove us to the airport at 7:30 A.M. Christmas Day. The gate agent said there'd been four people with emergencies in Florida, and they'd been given priority standby status.

It didn't matter. I knew that when that gate closed we'd be on the plane.

That afternoon, Andrew and I picked grapefruit from the tree next to the hot tub in the backyard of our friends' house in Florida. Nine days later, after sunning ourselves on Gulf beaches, exploring exotic wonders and following the Wisconsin marching band as they performed all over Tampa, we watched as the University of Wisconsin defeated Duke in the Hall of Fame Bowl on a beautiful, sunny, eighty-degree day.

Michael's last performance with the band was stellar.

But not quite as stellar as my faith in the Lord—who brings all things to pass.

Patricia Lorenz

The Plan

In his heart a man plans his course, but the Lord determines his steps.

PROVERBS 16:9

Bob and I pulled into Kirksville on a hot summer afternoon. "So what's the plan?" he asked.

"Plan? What plan? I thought *you* had a plan."

"I don't have a plan." He gave me the teasing, big-brother grin. "I thought *you* had a plan!"

We'd come to find our lost forty-five-year-old little brother. Keith had severed all ties with the family five years before. No one knew why. I suspected that when his wife left him without warning, he vowed that his broken heart would never be hurt again, and he let go of everyone he loved, simultaneously.

His absence, however, was breaking my mama's heart. Our mother personified unconditional love, but her letters to Keith were always unanswered and often returned as "addressee unknown."

"Let's start at the Wooden Nickel Café," I suggested. The last word on Keith had been three years ago, when a friend of a friend said he frequented the local café on Main Street. "We can have a late lunch there and ask if and when anyone's seen him. While we're eating, we can make a plan."

"Plan? I thought you had a plan?" Bob teased again.

It was easy to find the Wooden Nickel in the quaint downtown. We walked in and sat at one of the half-dozen tables. As we ordered the home-cooked daily special, we questioned the futility of our escapade.

I had driven from Colorado to Iowa to visit my six brothers and sisters and my mom. While I was there, Bob and I had concocted this day trip to find Keith. Bob's cows had gotten out earlier that morning, however, and by the time he got them back in, we were three hours behind schedule. We had even debated about canceling the four-hour drive altogether. But here we were in Kirksville.

"I'm not kidding myself," Bob said while we had our lunch. He tipped his farm-feed cap back on his head. "I think the chances of finding Keith are slim to none. But maybe we'll at least get some news about him we can share with Mom. There can't be that many independent carpenters in a town this size. We'll just ask around all day and into the night and ask some more tomorrow if we need to." Bob pulled a toothpick out of his denim shirt pocket and chewed on it. "He doesn't want to see us, you know."

"I know," I said glumly. "But we have to try. I can't explain it, Bob. I just know we're supposed to try."

"What'll you say if you see him?" Bob asked.

"I've rehearsed a dozen different things, yet I have no idea. I'm counting on God to give me the right words at the right time."

A kitchen door opened at the rear of the

café—and in walked Keith.

I grabbed an open menu and held it in front of my face.

"Oh dear God, Bob! It's Keith!" I hissed. "Don't turn around—he'll see you and I don't know what he'll do!"

Bob stared at me in disbelief. "You're sure it's him?"

"He's thinner than the last time I saw him, his hair is graying, but that's our Keithy."

"He likely won't be glad to see us," Bob whispered.

"What if he runs?"

"He can't run faster than me," Bob smirked.

I looked at Bob's receding gray hairline. "Right."

Keith was carrying on a quiet conversation with the man at the next table. Bob and I decided to wait until Keith's food was served before we approached him—maybe if he was eating, he wouldn't leave.

When the waiter placed a burger and fries in front of Keith, I signaled to Bob: "This is it!" Keith didn't see us get up and walk six steps to his table. I sat next to him, put my arm on his shoulder and said, "Can I buy you lunch?"

Keith turned to see me with shock—almost terror—on his face.

"What are you doing here?" he asked curtly.

"We came to have lunch with you," I said, my heart beating in my temples.

"Nothin' to do on the farm," Bob grinned. "So we decided to take a drive—and find you."

The waitress was obviously confused as she delivered our food to Keith's table. Keith politely introduced us to her and her husband behind the counter. The owners, he said. Then he finally forced a smile and said to me, "How're the kids?"

I began chattering like a chipmunk about our three grown children, adding funny stories of misadventures. These reminded Bob of mischievous antics we shared on the farm and Keith laughed with us as we recounted them.

I ate my sandwich in tiny slow bites, fearing that when the meal ended, so would the moment.

Then I could suppress it no longer. "You

seemed to have let us go, and we don't know why. Did any of us say or do anything?"

"No," Keith snapped.

"Christmas isn't the same without you. We miss you so much."

"I don't need that in my life anymore." His voice was terse.

"Mom went to Africa," I beamed.

"No kiddin'?" He smiled again. So I jabbered about tales of Mom bouncing along in a Jeep in Nairobi.

Then I nibbled while he told us about his work. He was remodeling the back room of the café into a bar and lounge. He always ate in the kitchen—he didn't know why he had come into the dining area today.

"Want to see what I do?" he asked.

Proudly he took us through the back kitchen door and into the lounge, filled with saws, lumber and tools. Small strips of inlaid wood fanned in a beautiful pattern on the wall. Bob and I marveled at the mastery of his work as he showed us around.

Too soon Keith said, "Well, I better get to work."

"Can I call you?" I ventured.

"Sure."

"Can I write you?"

"Sure."

With his carpenter's pencil, he scribbled his address and phone number on scratch paper. I wondered if they were true—if I'd ever see him again.

He shook Bob's hand, slapped him on the back, then pulled him into a bear hug.

He kissed me and held me to his chest. As I left the room, I turned to look back and said, "I love you, Keith."

His lips silently mouthed, "And I love you." As we headed home to tell Mom, Bob and I giggled and laughed.

"I'm so glad your cows got out and we were late, or we'd have missed him!"

"Can you believe he just came walking in there?"

We recounted every word and moment shared with our brother—so grateful that the Mighty Someone had a plan.

LeAnn Thieman

*

Love Bugs

Along unfamiliar paths I will guide them.
ISAIAH 42:16

My father-in-law leaned against his garden hoe and in his gentle voice warned, "If you don't do something with those bugs, you won't have any potatoes!" It was the summer of 1981, and we had just planted our first garden after moving to the farm from the big city of Toronto. Not having any gardening experience, I'd thought I could just plant and harvest. I didn't know there would be many long hours spent in the hot summer sun before we would reap what we had sown.

Standing at the edge of the garden, looking down those long rows of potatoes, I felt very inadequate beside my father-in-law who had been a farmer all of his life. I wondered, *Should I tell him I know nothing about getting rid of potato bugs?*

As if reading my thoughts, he said he would buy me a bag of potato bug poison when he went to town, and all I would have to do is dust the potato leaves with the powder. It wasn't long before I saw his truck coming back down our lane. Though I had seen him dusting in his own garden in his shirtsleeves, I read the instructions and precautions on the bag and donned long pants, a long-sleeved shirt, rubber boots, gloves, cap and mask. Up and down the rows I went on a hot summer afternoon dusting the rows with white powder. A week later the bugs were just as bad. We offered our two small sons a penny for each bug they could pick. After they filled a gallon ice-cream bucket, their interest dwindled. So again I went through the same dusting procedure over and over all summer, wondering, *Why did God make potato bugs?*

After we harvested our first crop of potatoes, I forgot all about the bugs. That is until planting time came around again. How I dreaded the idea of putting poison on our potatoes—organic gardening is what we had been dreaming about in the city. The second summer I decided it was time to tell Grandpa I would do away with dusting the potatoes forever. I took my gallon ice-cream bucket to the garden and began picking bugs.

I was surprised when one morning Grampie joined me there, with his own bucket and a shingle. "It will be easier this way," he told me. "Just tap the leaves gently and the bugs will fall into the bucket." Together we went up and down the rows. When I went back to the garden after supper, Grampie was there again. When we finished our garden we went to his garden. The next morning I looked out the kitchen window wondering if he would come again. Sure enough, I saw his truck coming down the lane. I met him at the garden, and with our buckets and shingles, we started down the rows. As we began our chore, Grampie began telling me a story.

"I remember when . . ." and with each row we walked, Grampie told me stories of the river, stories of how the Lawsons settled here, stories of his mother and father, stories of what it was like when he was a boy and how farming was in days gone by. Every now and then one of us would stop, wipe the sweat from our brows and say, "What good are these bugs anyway?" and then continue on.

Each gardening season, Grampie and I continued picking potato bugs. As his steps grew slower it took twice as long to finish a row but the, "I remember when . . ." stories became even more precious.

It wasn't long before my daughter Melanie joined us in our quest to rid the garden of potato bugs, and even at the age of eighty, there were not many days that Grampie didn't join us in the potato rows. One day Melanie asked, "Grampie, why did God make potato bugs?"

He replied, "I don't know, Melanie. They are nothing but a bother."

Then came the summer his cancer progressed. One evening as I went alone to his garden, he called from his lawn chair. I left my bucket in the rows and joined him at the front of the house. The river that he loved so much was calm and peaceful that evening and we sat for a long time as he told me still more river stories. We wondered where we would sell our beans tomorrow and discussed those useless potato bugs.

The next summer Melanie and I were alone in the garden.

Early mornings and late evenings found us there planning our days, wondering where she would spend her gardening money and daydreaming about the mountains. Every now and then one of us would say, "Remember when Grampie . . ." and more often than not, we would straighten our tired backs and scorn the potato bugs.

By the summer of 1999, Melanie was in Vancouver. I stood at the edge of the garden alone. With bucket and shingle in hand I started down the first row, and from days gone by I heard, "I remember when . . ." Only now I have my own memory stories. I remembered days spent with Grampie as we formed a rare and wonderful friendship, and days spent with Melanie as she daydreamed about life and the mountains.

I've planted my first garden of the new century, and this morning I start on the potato rows with a small boy at my side.

My four-year-old nephew Jordan is visiting from Sherbrooke, Quebec. He only speaks French and understands very little of what I say to him, but he understands that I love him very deeply. So when I hand him a bucket and a shingle, he anticipates that Auntie has something exciting in store for him. We start down the first row, Jordan on one side and me on the other. As he reaches across the row with wonder in his eyes, he tucks his small hand in mine. I spot a bug and drop it in his bucket. He looks up surprised and chatters away in French. I explain to him in English why we have to pick these bugs. I continue to find more bugs and drop them in his bucket. He is now intent on finding some for himself—his little head close to the plants, searching. We continue down the rows, delighting in his ability to find as many bugs as he can. He bursts with excitement over all those bugs in his bucket—and so do I.

I finally know why God made potato bugs.

Darlene Lawson

A Small Unsteady Light

Jesus said, "Let the little children come to me, and do not hinder them, for the kingdom of heaven belongs to such as these."

MATTHEW 19:14

My mother insisted one of us had to stay with the Turners, holidays or not. They should not be left alone. They were not only friends and neighbors, but belonged to our church, and Mrs. Turner, as far as anyone knew, had never refused a request to help anyone.

Now her family had been stricken, and my mother was determined to do whatever it took to stand by them. "It breaks my heart that they have to suffer this way," she said.

"We'll do our Christmas early. I'm not leaving Jeremy and Ruth to struggle through Christmas. Each of you can spend a day there now and I will go over on Christmas day. Then you all will just have to fend for yourselves."

So three days before Christmas I went to stay with the Turners. I was to answer phones and do errands—whatever I was asked to do.

Their house, just two doors from ours, was the most sorrowful place I'd ever been. There were no Christmas decorations and hardly any lights on in the whole house. I wanted to go through the house and turn on all the lights, but that wasn't up to me to do. I answered phone calls and cleaned up the kitchen. They ate mostly fried chicken or meatloaf or vegetable soup brought in by friends and neighbors. They rarely talked because there was nothing to say.

Almost a week earlier their son, Skip, who was nine, had taken his old bike to Jim Nelson's house to practice carols with Jim and two other boys in their quartet. He broke his chain as he struggled to pedal up their steep drive. When they were finished practicing, Punky Harkins rode Skip home on his bike. Fifteen minutes later, Skip was dead. They'd skidded on the streetcar tracks on Harrison Avenue and Skip was thrown. His head struck a piece of frozen sludge, fallen from a passing car. He never opened his eyes again.

Now, four days after the funeral, Ruth Turner often sat alone in the kitchen drinking coffee. The Turners had sort of a playroom with an old couch downstairs, and I was down there on Christmas Eve reading when I heard Jeremy Turner come in the front door. I heard him go into the kitchen. He moved around a little, then I heard him say, "Gonna make coffee. Want some?"

"I have some," she said. Her voice sounded as though it hadn't been used for a long, long time. I knew she was sitting at the oak table, hunched over, head bowed, looking at the picture of Skip she kept with her all the time.

Then Mr. Turner said, "I'm going to put that away."

"Give that back, Jeremy. It's mine!" She screamed this at him. That sound made me afraid and I didn't know what to do. Then she said, "If you'd bought him a bike when he wanted it! If you had just once listened!"

"Stop it, Ruth. Stop it. I loved him as much as you."

Then there was scuffling, and the crash of glass, and then no sound at all. None. I did not know what to do. I waited until I was certain they'd left the kitchen and then crept upstairs. The frame the picture of Skip had been in was smashed and there was glass all over the floor. I began to clean up the mess.

I could hear Mrs. Turner crying in their bedroom. It was a soft sound that somehow reminded me of a bird's wings. I cleaned up the glass, wrapped it in paper and put it in the trash. I thought of calling my mom, but the worst seemed to be over and there was nothing she could do. Nothing anyone could do.

I decided to make hot chocolate, just in case. I don't know what made me do it, except we always had it at our house when everyone needed to calm down. As I was heating the milk, I heard the sound. It was faint and strange. The sound was coming from the Turners' yard. It was soft and shaky—the sound of small boys trying to sing carols before the dark face of the Turners' house.

Then Mr. and Mrs. Turner came downstairs. He came first and she a few moments later. I moved back against the living room wall trying to stay out of the way. They stood together in the darkness, waiting, I thought, for the singing to end. But it didn't. The boys sang and sang until the Turners finally went to the door.

Mr. Turner turned the light on in the hallway and then quickly opened the door. On the lawn stood three small boys. Last year, there had been four. Last year they'd had to pretend they did not know they were going to be caroling. It always had to be a surprise in our neighborhood.

The three boys stood there holding candles, the tiny flames throwing a small unsteady light. The boys were trying to sing "O Little Town of Bethlehem." Their breath frosted in the winter air and rose above their heads like smoke. Mr. Turner looked down at his wife who was clutching her robe at the throat. She took his hand and shivered so badly I could see it. She leaned against him, and he put his arm around her shoulder. Then we all saw in the flickering candlelight, a small boy standing in the snow, trying to sing. Punky Harkins was trying his best to sing although his entire body was shaken with the terrible sorrow he must have felt.

Mrs. Turner put her hands over her eyes and said softly, "Oh Lord, Lord." I held my breath, hoping that the darkness in her would break, that somehow she would not feel so alone. She stood, with her husband, for a long time, leaning into his body. And then he, in a gesture so gentle, so soft, that it seemed to come from someplace he had never before touched, he reached his hand to her face and guided her gaze outward to where the three boys of Skip's quartet sang in the cold winter air—"and in the dark street shineth, an everlasting light."

She looked out at them and then she raised her head. "Oh, that poor little boy," she said, "That little boy. To think of how he must feel!"

And she ran down the walk, through the sparkling snow and swept him up in her arms.

Walker Meade

Meeting God at 30,000 Feet

Humanity is never so beautiful as when praying for forgiveness, or else forgiving another.

JEAN PAUL RICHTER

I did some dumb things in junior high school. I think it just comes with the territory. But one particularly dumb thing involved a theft. I didn't steal money or shoplift, and I didn't take anyone's boyfriend. I simply stole a few votes.

The scene of the crime was journalism class, where those of us on the yearbook staff sat counting ballots for the school superlatives contest. Suddenly someone yelled out, "Caron! It looks like you may get enough votes to win Most Talented."

Until that moment, I had been the epitome of average. Winning a category in the superlatives contest would skyrocket my approval rating at Glenridge Junior High. I was eking out a social existence because my friends had friends who were cool. Like a mere feeder fish, I hovered close to the big fish in hopes of sucking some algae off them.

I soon found out, however, that I was not the only one up for Most Talented. Trailing close behind me was Cindy, our school's guitar-playing singer. Cindy had real talent. She was even asked to sing her original song, "Beauty," at a school assembly. My only claim to fame was the pen and ink drawings I did on notebooks and book covers. Hardly a class went by that I didn't get at least one request for "Judy & Johnny 4-Ever," or "S. M. loves T. P."

Clearly, my talent was no match for Cindy's. Someone important once said, "The pen is mightier than the sword." But no one ever mentioned how the pen would do against the guitar. Guitars were big deals. I knew if I didn't do something fast, I would live my whole life in obscurity.

So, while votes were being tallied for other categories, I secretly grabbed a handful of uncounted ballots and tossed them in the trash. I was pretty sure no one saw me. I should have felt guilty, but I didn't. At the end of the day, I had won. And suddenly the demand for notebook art increased a good 40 percent.

Why it took God fifteen years to confront me on this, I'll never know. But it was He who brought it up one morning in my prayer time. By then we were on a first name basis, and He had full permission to speak to me about anything that bothered Him. Here is an abbreviated version of our conversation:

Me: God, I want to be all I can be for You. I've searched my heart for anything that might be standing in the way of this, and I've come up empty. I think I've dealt with all the sins I've ever committed. But I'll just sit here and wait for You to go through your files and see if You have something there I may have left out.

God: Well, there was that time in junior high school.

Me: Which time?

God: Most Talented?

Me: You saw that? It was such a long time ago. Surely You have a statute of limitations or some kind of cutoff date for people who do dumb things prior to high school.

God: Not really.

Me: But, I'm 1,200 miles away. No telling where Cindy is. Do You realize the difficulty I would have in finding her? Okay, here's what I'll do. If one day I'm walking down the street and I happen to see her, I'll know You sent her and I'll make things right with her. Fair enough?

God: Fair enough.

I felt pretty safe. I hadn't seen Cindy in years. The odds of running into her in another state were microscopic.

Six months later, my husband and I were racing through the airport trying to catch a plane. When we reached the door of the 747, it had just been shut. My husband, forever the determined optimist, banged on the door as the noise of the engines accelerated. Suddenly, a nice flight attendant with exceptional hearing came to our rescue and opened the door.

We made our way to the back of the plane, comparing our tickets to the numbers overhead until we found a match. I plopped down in the middle seat assigned to me. Using my polite voice I said "Hello" to a woman next to me who was looking out the window. When she returned my greeting, adrenaline shot through me. In unison we both exclaimed, "Oh, my gosh! I can't believe it!"

There was Cindy, the guitar-playing singer.

A boxing match began inside me. From one corner came the feeling of someone who had just been given a million dollars. And from the other came the emotions of a hunted felon. Immediately I began carrying on two conversations, one on the surface with Cindy, the other internally with God.

Me: You actually found her! This is an outright miracle! I can't believe You are forcing me to do this. You really are into the details, aren't You?

God: Yes.

From takeoff to landing, Cindy and I chattered away but all I could think of was how, out of the hundreds of thousands of people on airplanes that day, God looked for a needle in a haystack, found it, threaded it and placed it in my hand.

My palms started to sweat. I swallowed hard. No use stalling any longer. It was time to let Cindy in on the whole story. "Cindy," I said. "You're not going to believe this, but it's no accident we met today. Several months ago, I promised God I would make things right if our paths should ever cross again."

As I explained, Cindy laughed. She easily forgave me. It barely fazed her. I felt like scolding God for orchestrating such an ordeal. Then a familiar quote popped into my mind, "To whom much is given, much is required." God knew that if I'd confess a small matter from the past, He could trust me with greater responsibilities in the future.

I felt far from the epitome of average.

Caron Loveless

Tammy and the
Diamond Dress

Sitting on the flowered print couch, I paged through the Kissees' family album: there was nine-year-old Tammy, ten-year-old Tammy, eleven-year-old Tammy. Then I looked across the room at twelve-year-old Tammy playing checkers with her father. Her long blonde hair was gone; the radiation had left only a wisp of fuzz on her head. Her fair complexion was now a chalky gray. The skeleton-like limbs made her appear weak and breakable.

Tammy caught a side glimpse of me staring, and she figured out pretty quickly that I had to be comparing her to the robust girl sitting astride the black horse in the picture.

She smiled at me as if to say, "It's okay. I'll be that girl again someday."

My four-year-old daughter Kimberly leaned over Tammy's shoulder to watch her next move on the game board. "I think you should jump the black checker with the red one, Tammy." Tammy laughed, touching her dark curls with envy. "I *am* the black checker."

We met the Kissee family a year earlier when they began attending our small country church, soon after Tammy had been diagnosed with liver cancer. They joined the congregation, and we all began to pray daily for a healing miracle.

There was something so ethereal about Tammy. Kimberly couldn't resist her and became her shadow. Often Tammy felt weary from treatment, but she somehow managed to add strength to her patience in dealing with this admiring fan. Tammy had two older brothers, so she treated Kimberly as a welcomed younger sister. With their heads together, one nearly bald and the other thick with lustrous curls, they paged through the children's Bible.

One day as I sewed, Kimberly said, "I

need a diamond dress to wear for special occasions, like to parties and weddings and funerals." I flinched at her last word. Tammy laughed and seemed to understand something I could not grasp.

"Why funerals?" I could not meet Tammy's eyes.

"Because when people die they go home to heaven. I really need a dress for that celebration!"

Monday morning, Kimberly and I sorted through stacks and rows of fabric in the basement of an old Ben Franklin store.

"Here it is!" she exclaimed, holding up some purple cloth with a colorful jelly-bean print on it. "Diamonds!"

"Honey, those are jelly beans."

"No, they are diamonds, beautiful colored diamonds."

I looked at the material for a long time, trying to see what Kimberly saw, but finally gave up. I asked for two yards to be cut, picked out matching thread and paid my money. All week I struggled with making my daughter's diamond dress. To make it fancier I sewed on a lace collar and dotted it with rhinestones. Kimberly was happy with the result; she saw diamonds, I saw jelly beans.

Christmas was festive at church with a wonderful program and platters of carefully prepared food. Tammy admitted she felt awkward around girls her own age, as they didn't quite know how to act toward the girl who looked so different from them. So she remained by her little four-year-old friend and was a wonderful help in serving the food.

I thought I detected a little color crawling back into Tammy's wan cheeks. *Surely she will recover and be just fine.* I said another silent prayer for the hundredth, the thousandth, the millionth time.

I watched Tammy out of the corner of my eye all evening. She checked plates and cups, making sure everyone had enough to eat and drink, and served more when needed. She seated the elderly in the most comfortable chairs. I saw her push back the constant fatigue she experienced in order to help turn the pages for the pianist's music. At last, she sat with the children gathered about her feet, leading them in Christmas songs, listening intently to their stories. She was a young girl who was not self-absorbed in makeup and boyfriends. She was a young girl absorbed in helping others.

Two days after Christmas, we received a call from Tammy's parents. She had been rushed to the hospital. Walking into her room, I noticed how small she looked among the bed sheets. Her mother rubbed her forehead and smiled into the blue eyes that were heavy with sleep. My husband and I stood by her bed, along with her parents and brothers. Although we had prayed for healing, God performed His own miracle and just before midnight took Tammy home to live with Him in heaven.

The members of the church dreaded the funeral of one so young. We seem to understand and accept better the death of someone elderly who has lived a long and full life. This young life slipping away from us, however, made our own mortality seem more brittle. And there were the nagging questions: Had we failed Tammy in not believing hard enough, in not praying long enough?

I held my four-year-old daughter's hand as we walked up to the old oak casket. Tammy appeared as if she had gotten ready for church and then simply laid down for a quick rest among her favorite toys. I squeezed Kimberly's hand tighter. If she got too close to the casket, would death snatch her too? Sensing my fears, Mr. Kissee picked Kimberly up into his arms so she could clearly see Tammy's face.

"She is at peace now. See, no more pain on her face," he told her.

Kimberly looked into the pain-filled father's eyes and then nodded seriously, turning her attention back to her friend.

"Thanks for helping me be quiet in church," my daughter whispered to her. "See, I wore my diamond dress for you today. You knew how important it was. I am so happy that you can see heaven. Save me a seat next to you."

During the service, Tammy's parents sat close together holding hands, their grieving sons on either side. The pastor spoke, "This is not the end but the beginning for Tammy. Let her beginning be a new beginning for us as well. Let's finish what she has started, and may it be a work in progress."

It was true. Tammy left us with so much. She set her own needs aside to help others.

She cheerfully illustrated to my impressionable daughter, to children yet to be shaped, and to adults set in their ways, how to be of service to others when pain and tiredness are your greatest enemies.

That night I tucked my own little daughter into her bed, thinking that Tammy would never be tucked into hers again. Kim looked at me with concern. Her tiny finger brushed away one of my tears.

"Mommy, when I close my eyes I can see Tammy. She has her long blonde hair back and wears a beautiful dress with stones all over it. I think her diamond dress is even prettier than mine," Kimberly whispered while pointing to her jelly-bean dress hanging in the closet.

I closed my eyes too. Yes, I can imagine Tammy with her long hair and pink, glowing complexion. I think she is probably wearing her own diamond dress as she gallops through the streets of heaven.

Robin Lee Shope

Ivy's Cookies

Blessed are those who can give without remembering and take without forgetting.

ELIZABETH BIBESCO

The clank of the metal door and the echo of their footsteps rang in the ears of Ivy and Joanne as they walked down the dingy corridor behind the prison guard toward the "big room." The aroma of Ivy's homemade chocolate chip cookies wasn't enough to override the stench of ammonia from the recently mopped floor, or the bitterness and anger that hung in the air. Women's Correctional Institute was not the kind of place where most seventeen-year-olds go for an outing, but Ivy had a mission.

She didn't know what she was getting into, but she had to try. With trembling fingers, she had dialed the number for an appointment at the prison. Warden Baylor was receptive to Ivy's desire to visit and referred her to Joanne, another teen who had also expressed interest.

"How do we do this?" Ivy asked.

"Who knows? Maybe homemade cookies would break the ice," Joanne suggested.

So they baked their cookies and came bearing gifts to strangers.

"I put almonds in these," Ivy rambled nervously as they moved along. "The dough was gummier than usual . . ."

"Don't chatter," the guard snapped. "It gets the prisoners riled."

The harsh words made Ivy jump and her heart pound. She walked the rest of the distance in silence.

"Okay. Here we are," the guard grunted, keys rattling. "You go in. I'll lock the door behind you. Be careful what you say. They have a way of using your words against you. You have fifteen minutes. Holler if you have any trouble." Ivy noted the prisoners' orange jumpsuits and felt overdressed.

Maybe we shouldn't have worn heels, she thought. *They probably think we're snobs.*

Remembering the guard's admonition, the girls put the cookies on the table next to plastic cups of juice, without saying a word. Some prisoners leaned against the wall; others stood around watching, studying, thinking, staring. Nobody talked. Ivy smiled at one of the women, who scowled back. From then on, Ivy avoided eye contact with the inmates. After five minutes of strained silence, Joanne whispered, "Let's move away from the table. Maybe they'll come over."

As they stepped back, one of the prisoners blurted out, "I'm gettin' a cookie." The others followed and began helping themselves. Soon they heard the rattle of keys. Time was up.

"What a relief to get out of there," Joanne sighed as a gust of fresh air caressed their perspiring faces.

"Yeah," Ivy agreed. "But I have a strong feeling that we're not done. Would you be willing to go back?"

Joanne nodded with a half-smile. "How about Thursday after school?"

Week after week they came. And week after week the prisoners ate the cookies, drank the juice and stood around in silence. Gradually, antagonistic looks were replaced by an occasional smile. Still, Ivy couldn't bring herself to speak—not a word.

Then one Thursday, an evangelist walked in. Her step was sure, her chin was high and she glowed with the love of God. But she meant business. "I've come to pray with you," she announced to the inmates. "Let's make a circle."

Ivy was awed by the women's compliance. Only a few resisted. The others, although murmuring, inched their way toward the middle of the room and formed a lopsided circle, looking suspiciously at one another.

"Join hands," the evangelist instructed. "It's not gonna hurt you, and it'll mean more if you do." Slowly, some women clasped hands, others barely touched. "Now, bow your heads."

Except for the orange outfits, it could have been a church meeting.

"Okay. We're gonna pray," the evangelist continued, "and prayer is just like talking, only to God. I want to hear you tell the Lord one thing you're thankful for. Just speak it out. Don't hold back."

Ivy's palms were sweaty. *I can't pray aloud, Lord. I can't even talk to these women. I guess I should set an example, but they probably don't even like me—they probably think I'm better than they are because of my clothes.*

The words of an inmate jolted her from her thoughts.

"I'm thankful, God, for Miss Ivy bringing us cookies every week."

Another voice compounded the shock. "God, thanks for bringing a black lady to see us."

Ivy's eyes brimmed with tears as she heard, "Thank you, God, for these two young ladies giving their time every week, even though we can't do anything to pay them back."

One by one, every inmate in the circle thanked God for Ivy and Joanne. Then Joanne managed to utter a prayer of gratitude for the prisoners' words. But when it came Ivy's turn, she was too choked up to speak. Her eyes burned in humble remorse over how wrong she'd been about these women. She wished she could blow her nose, but the inmates were squeezing her hands so tightly, she resorted to loud sniffles and an occasional drip.

The following week, Ivy and Joanne returned, bright eyed, to find the prisoners talkative.

"Why do you bring us cookies every week?" a husky voice inquired from the corner of the room. When Ivy explained, the inmate inched a few steps closer. "Can you get me a Bible?" she asked. Others wanted to know more about the Jesus who inspires teenagers to visit prisoners.

A ministry was born from Ivy's cookies. What started as a silent act of kindness and obedience turned into a weekly Bible study at the prison, which eventually grew so big, it split into several groups that continue to this day. After Joanne married and moved away, Ivy continued to minister to the inmates alone for years. Eventually Prison Fellowship picked up the baton.

Ivy is a grandma now. Her radiance has increased over the years, and she brightens any room she enters. But last Thursday afternoon she indulged herself in a good cry. Curled up on the couch, wrapped in the afghan her daughter had made, she wept on the first anniversary of her daughter's death. "Her kids can live with me," Ivy had said. Now they napped as the doorbell rang.

A young woman, about seventeen, stood there with a plate of homemade cookies.

"Are you Ivy Jones?" she asked.

"Yes," she answered, dabbing her eyes with a wadded tissue.

"These are for you," the girl said as she handed the cookies to her. With a shy, sad smile, she turned to leave without another word.

"Thank you," Ivy whispered in a daze. The girl was halfway down the sidewalk when Ivy called out, "But why?"

"My grandmother gave me her Bible before she died last week, and her last words were, 'Find Ivy Jones and take her some homemade cookies.'"

Candy Abbott

Leadership Material

Generosity lies less in giving much than in giving at the right moment.

JEAN LA BRUYERE

I was new to the church the first time I went to a women's fellowship meeting. Had I known it was their night to reorganize their committees, I would have stayed home. Since then I read my church bulletin very carefully.

After explaining what the various guilds did, they asked everyone to choose which one they would be part of. I chose the Parish Guild. That committee sent out cards to new parents, the sick and the bereaved. They also provided food for the funeral suppers. I could do the cards. The food, if I had to cook it, would be a problem. I wondered how they felt about store-bought desserts.

I was about to raise that question when Lori asked if I wouldn't mind being chair. I stared at her like she had spoken Swahili. Then I told her I really was not leadership material. She smiled. It was a "pat-on-the-head-and-don't-worry-about-a-thing-dear" smile. Lori said, "Everyone will help. You only have to make the calls."

"Okay," I relented.

"It'll be fine," she reassured me.

And the first months were. I selected cards and sent them out. It was easy. It was a joy. Then someone died.

Helen, my pastor's wife, called me and told me. She said I was to call the family and ask if they wanted the guild to provide food for the gathering after the service. I practically dropped the phone. Nobody had told me I had to call the family. Nobody had told me that was part of my job.

I called. I was awful at it. I hemmed and hawed my way through the whole conversation, although I wanted to be so sensitive.

The day of the memorial service I stopped by church to check on the food. The guild women, as promised, had come through— three entrees, three salads, three desserts so far. I hoped that other people would bring food to the house. I left with my small daughter to do errands.

On my way home, I stopped by church to make sure that all the food had been picked up and taken to the house. The organ was playing as I passed the sanctuary. I looked at my watch. *This sure is a long service,* I thought as I rounded a corner. I nearly knocked Helen over. She was wearing her best black dress and practically running, her hands loaded with a huge silver platter.

I recognized the meatloaf entree on it. "They think the meal is here at the church," she whispered. "Pastor is stalling for time while we set up." The sound of a metal tray crashing to the floor echoed from the parish hall. Helen flinched.

Then she straightened. "I've started the coffee," she continued bravely. "The oven in the kitchen is on the fritz. I'm taking the meat home to warm it. I'll be back as soon as I can." I nodded like a person caught in a whirlwind—which I was.

"Nancy, did you tell them the meal was to be at their home?"

"I, I just assumed that . . ."

"Never mind," said that saintly woman, "it'll be all right." She dashed toward the parking lot.

I sighed and watched her departing figure. Holding my daughter's hand, I trudged across the patio to the kitchen. On the island counter were the three salads, the three desserts and the two entrees minus the meatloaf. I glanced over my shoulder, out the door. The church parking lot was nearly full.

God, what are we going to do? There must be over 100 people at the service. This is going to be a fiasco. I closed my eyes as if to shut out the future. The giant coffeepot perked away merrily. *How dare it?*

I set out the napkins and brought up plates from the cupboards. I removed the plastic wrap from the food containers and put serving spoons in them. The organ stopped playing. My stomach fluttered as footsteps and voices approached the kitchen.

People began streaming in. In their hands they carried green salads and macaroni salads and Jell-O salads, casseroles and sandwiches, bread and cold cuts, pies and cakes, plates of cookies and brownies. For a moment it was happy chaos as we found places for all the food. Then people lined up. Smiling graciously I stepped behind the counter and handed out coffee. I hoped that the tall people wouldn't notice that I was wearing blue jeans.

Later, as one of the daughters of the deceased was gathering up the remains of the leftover food she smiled. "It was great having this at the church," she said. "Mother was worrying and making herself sick over how she would ever get the house ready."

Her words filled me with awe. *God*, I thought, *You sure do move in mysterious ways.*

I managed the next funeral okay. Helen said pointedly, "Tell them, Nancy, that the meal is to be at their house." I did.

However, the funeral after that one found me dog-paddling in disaster again. While loading the food into my car, I broke a salad bowl and chipped a crockpot lid.

At the end of my one-year tenure as

Parish Guild chair, I heaved a sigh of relief. I hadn't gotten through unscathed, but it had all worked out. God had made it work out. I congratulated myself that I had done my bit as a leader and now could retreat into being a committee member.

Then the women's fellowship elected me president.

Nancy Ellen Hird

"Does our daily bread mean crust, too?"

And the Little Child
Shall Lead Them

As I sit on the porch watching my children play in the yard, my eyes turn to Jeremy, the youngest of our children, the baby. When we adopted Jeremy, knowing he would be physically and mentally delayed, we planned to teach him so much. However, as I watch him play, I realize God had another plan.

Jeremy climbs onto his older brother's *Star Wars* bike. He does this with such confidence, I'm sure he'd be pedaling down the sidewalk by now if he were just two inches taller. Instead, he straddles the back tire and grips the handlebars, turning them back and forth, willing the bicycle to move.

As I watch him attempt this challenge, I vow to forget my own weaknesses and not let fear of failure stop me when facing a challenge of my own.

Out of the corner of his eye, eyes that are supposedly visually impaired, Jeremy spots the yellow and blue Little Tikes grocery cart on the sidewalk. Sitting on his bottom, he moves easily across the walkway and begins to scoot down the five steps that will lead him to the cart he continues to eye. Stair climbing is not a practiced skill, though he masters the downward descent with ease. His physical therapist would be proud. I am proud.

His determination inspires me. I vow to remember his determination the next time something difficult stands between me and the object of my desires.

He walks with pride across the sidewalk. Though he can't walk on his own, he looks graceful pushing the grocery cart full of wet leaves that helps him balance on two feet. He turns to me and smiles as he takes one careful step after another. When he hits a dip in the sidewalk that stops him from continuing his journey, he attempts to push the cart out of the rut on his own, but finally decides that, without help, he can go no further. He looks over his shoulder, sees his three-year-old brother digging in the rain-softened dirt, and in perfect Jeremy-ese, yells, "OoooohAaaaaaah."

Keyen, who understands Jeremy's language well, walks to the cart, gives it a firm push that releases it from the rut, and Jeremy is happily on his way.

As I watch, I vow to swallow my pride and ask for help the next time life's journey sticks me in a rut I can't get out of on my own.

Jeremy doesn't travel far when the right blue wheel of his grocery cart veers off the edge of the sidewalk. Before I can reach him, he tumbles to the ground. Though at first he is too stunned to respond, seconds later, he is sitting up, rubbing his head and letting the tears fall freely down his cheeks. I pick him up, hold him tightly and whisper, "You're okay, buddy," over and over in his ear. He accepts my comfort for a moment, then pushes himself out of my arms to get back to the challenging journey that awaits him.

As he strolls on, I vow to remember that

when life knocks me down, I'll feel sorry for myself for only a moment. I'll heed the encouragement of those who love me, and I'll get right back up and move on.

I stay a few steps behind Jeremy so I can catch him if he falls. As I walk, I'm reminded that there is someone beside me, too. I vow to remember God in my prayers tonight and thank Him for being there to catch me when I fall.

Jeremy has only walked a few feet when something else catches his observant eye and he's on his hands and knees searching for the treasure he knows is there. He picks up a rock. A plain, ordinary rock if you ask me, but Jeremy sees something else. He smiles at the beautiful rock he holds in his hand. He looks at it closely, touches it to his cheek and again shows his pleasure in his familiar language, "Oooohhhhhuuuuhhhh." He looks at it one more time, then tosses it aside and crawls to the grocery cart that enables him to continue his stroll. As he walks ahead, I pick up the rock he discarded and discover that it's not as plain and ordinary as I'd first thought. Shiny little specks catch the sunlight to make a beautiful sparkle, and when I touch it to my cheek, it's smooth and cool.

As I put the rock in my pocket, I vow to remember to take time to discover the small treasures that may go unnoticed if I travel too quickly on the path of life. I vow to uncover the beauty in what may at first seem plain and ordinary.

By now, Jeremy has walked all the way to the chalk line, three houses from ours, that says, "Stop Here." Although I know he doesn't understand, I explain that we've reached our boundary and turn him and his cart the opposite way. The journey home seems quicker, and with less distractions.

As we near our front steps, I fully expect Jeremy to pass our house and head toward the park across the street. But, as always, he is full of surprises. He stops in front of our house, lets go of his beloved grocery cart and turns to me with arms held high. I lift him over my head. He squeals with delight.

As we walk up the steps and into the yard, I vow to never forget the way home, or that home contains something far more valuable than what may look exciting across the street. As I tell my other children to put their toys away so we can go in for lunch, a neighbor stops to chat. She jokingly mentions that our efforts to grow grass in our front yard are failing. I smile, knowing that as long as there are active children at home, we will never have a beautifully landscaped yard. My neighbor smiles at Jeremy who is already smiling through the drool dripping down his chin. Knowing that Jeremy is adopted, my neighbor says the same thing that we hear so often, "What a lucky boy."

I smile and respond the same way I have a hundred times before, "We're the lucky ones." We say our good-byes and turn to go our separate ways. My neighbor says to no one in particular, but loud enough for me to hear, "What a wonderful family. They'll teach him so much."

And, as my precious children and I walk into our house, I realize that Jeremy has already taught us everything that's important in life.

Dawn Nowakoski

The Miracle of Medjugorje

Miracles—whether prophetically or of other sorts—always occur in connection with some message from heaven, and are intended by God as a seal, or endorsement of the messenger and His word.

ALOYSIUS MCDONOUGH

Mom always had a great devotion to the Virgin Mary. She didn't believe that Mary could answer prayers, but that she was an intercessor to her son, Jesus. While my mom was raising eight kids, she likely thought she needed all the interceding she could get!

Each of us had a rosary, and my mother taught us to say the Hail Mary on each bead. A statue of the Blessed Virgin sat prominently on the buffet, and fresh flowers adorned her, especially in May.

Mom read us stories of how Mary had appeared to a young girl in Lourdes, France, and to children in Guadeloupe, Mexico. Then in the 1980s, Mom told her then-grown children new accounts of Mary appearing to youngsters in Medjugorje, Bosnia. Intrigued by the modern-day miracle, my mom bought books about it, subscribed to the Medjugorje magazine, attended seminars on the topic—and bought a ticket to Bosnia.

I've always said that my mother was eighty going on fifty. In spite of several old fractures, numerous surgeries and a mild heart condition, she taught religious education classes, gave slide show presentations of her safari to Africa and drove "old people" to their doctors' appointments.

"I don't know if I can climb the mountain," my mom said, "but I just want to go. I can't explain it—I just need to go. And I'm not going so I can ask for a miracle," she added emphatically.

But many who went, did. There were hundreds of accounts of miraculous healings and faith conversions at Medjugorje.

Her tour group arrived in Medjugorje late one damp November night. The next morning they learned their scheduled trek had been postponed, due to the rain and slippery slopes. One younger man who had made the trip twice before, said he could wait no longer—he was climbing the mile-long mountain path right then. My mother said, "Me, too."

So with a pin in her ankle, five metal rods in her back and a song in her heart, my mom set off for the climb. She was surprised to see the trail was only jagged rocks. Step by cautious step, she hiked upward—past a woman even older than she, kneeling in prayerful meditation, and past a half-dozen rowdy ten-year-old boys, running and yelping with joy. Soon they raced ahead of her and later she came upon them again, kneeling in quiet prayer.

Within two hours, my mother stood in wonder and awe at the top of the mountain, on the very site the Virgin had appeared. She knelt in the sprinkling rain and did what she always did—she prayed for her children.

The trek down was even more difficult than the ascent. Each step on the rugged rocks jarred her as she struggled to find stable footing. The rain intensified as they wound their way through the foreign streets. Mom returned to the group, soaking wet but marveling that, not only had she made the climb, she had done so without her usual pain. "Maybe that was the miracle," she mused.

The next day was just another day in war-torn Bosnia, but it was Thanksgiving Day in the States—and the tour guide had a plan to make it a day of thanksgiving in Medjugorje, too. On every tour the staff purchased and distributed groceries and supplies to the most needy in the community. All of the dozen members of my mother's tour group readily offered to contribute to the fund and help with the deliveries.

Their large bus stopped at the grocery store where the ordered bags of goods were loaded into the back. Carefully, the group counted the twenty-four, garbage-sized bags. Local church and government officials had made a list of those in most desperate need, and the bus headed off to share thanksgiving with them.

The first stop was a shanty with the roof partially blown off. Mom and her new friends filed past damaged household furniture sitting on the dirt lawn and entered the one room the family of four occupied. Laughing, smiling and crying, the old couple accepted the food and supplies. Two young boys in clean ragged clothes chattered their gratitude, while their toddler brother clung to his grandma's leg, whining and fussing. Their parents had been tortured and killed by the enemy, the tour guide explained. Yet the family jubilantly hugged my mom and her crew good-bye as they headed off to the next stop.

The bus driver seemed to have the route and stops memorized from the many trips before. At the next run-down house, a wrinkled old woman in a headscarf stood waving from her cluttered front porch. As the group entered, she placed her hands on each of their faces and kissed them, one by one, thanking them in her native tongue. Inside she gathered them in one of the two rooms left standing in her once-three bedroom home. There she prayed, not for herself, but for her guests.

The driver stopped next at a ramshackle house at the end of a lane, and before the tour guide could say, "They aren't on our list this time," a man and two young boys raced toward the bus clapping for joy. At the directive of the tour guide, the bus pulled away.

"Can't we please leave them some food," my mother politely protested as she looked back at the family waving sadly.

"We only had twenty-four bags to start with," the guide explained, her voice thick with sorrow. "We have other families waiting for these—we promised them."

The team sat, despondent, until the driver stopped at yet another war-damaged home. A couple who looked years older than my mom were caring for two grown sons, each suffering from a wasting muscular disease. Yet their faith and joy exceeded even that of the team as they crowded the entire group into their tiny kitchen to pray—then insisted that they all share in the food the old woman had prepared for them.

And so went the day, house after house, family after family, each physically destitute and spiritually wealthy.

"That's twenty-four!" the guide said as she checked the last name off the list after the final stop.

"No, twenty-three," someone corrected. "There is one bag of food left."

Dumbfounded, the group looked in the back of the bus to see one lone bag of food.

"We all counted the bags and the people on the list three times," one member said breathlessly.

"There was no error," the guide said. Then, smiling, she asked, "Are there loaves and fish in that bag?"

The entire team stared at each other—first in confusion, then in awe, then in elation. They cheered, "Let's go!"

The bus returned to the ramshackle house at the end of the lane, and the man and two boys raced out, as if they were expecting them.

LeAnn Thieman
Dedicated to Mom, Berniece Duello

Do You Believe in God?

Jesus said to the woman, "Your faith has saved you; go in peace."

LUKE 7:50

"Mom, I need pictures!" Marie exclaimed. "The bus is going to be here in fifteen minutes, and Mr. Martinez says I need at least ten."

Mr. Martinez says. Well, we surely can't disappoint him.

"Here, look through these," I shoved a box at my youngest daughter and raced off to help find the shoe my older son had "lost."

When I returned my attention to Marie's picture problem, I noticed tears on her cheek. "We'll get enough pictures, honey," I assured her. "Don't worry. If you miss the bus, your dad can drop you off on the way to work."

"It's not that, Mom; it's this." She flipped around the picture she had been staring at. For the first time in a long time, I saw flecks of fear in her ice blue eyes.

Fear doesn't cloud Marie's thoughts very often. She is my adventurous one. "Anything they can do, I can do better," is her motto. She can jump farther, climb higher. She can fly! She is invincible. Just ask her.

As Marie looked at that picture I knew she remembered the horrible day fear wracked her mind and body. That day, Marie realized she could die.

I sat and soothed my nine-year-old daughter, drawing her trembling body into the lap she had clearly outgrown. I looked at the scene that invoked her tears: a crumpled red station wagon resting atop a flatbed tow truck.

"Mom, how come we didn't get hurt?" she asked, awe thick in her voice. "I don't understand how the windows on my side broke, the roof smashed in and we didn't even get hurt."

Marie wasn't the only one with that question. Everyone had voiced it that day.

It was a typical Wednesday. I was on my way home from a meeting at church with my daughter and three-year-old nephew. I had decided to try a new shortcut and turned off on a dirt road flanked by neat rows of corn. The curve ahead surprised me, as did the sight of the deep canal. Suddenly we hit a patch of gravel and the tires loosened their grip on the road. I had no control.

"Oh God, help us," I prayed out loud, as our car hurled down the ravine, ricocheted off the steep embankment, bounced force-fully in the water and then came to rest. *The children! Oh God, please let the children be all right.* Just then they began to cry. *Thank you.*

I looked back. Both kids appeared to be okay. "Are you two hurt?" They both shook their heads, no.

"My hice, my hice," my little nephew cried.

"What?"

"He spilled his ice," Marie translated for me.

If that's all he's worried about, he can't be injured too badly.

I took stock of the situation. The car was perched on a small shelf of land jutting out into the water. We couldn't stay there. We were hidden from the road above. Even if a car happened along, they wouldn't be able to spot us. And if the water rose just a little bit, we would be in trouble.

"Come on kids, let's get out of here." The driver's side of the car opened into the water, so after I struggled to release the seat belt and car-seat buckles, I herded both children out the passenger door. I gave them the once over. Shards of safety glass tangled their hair and glinted in the sun. But no scratches, no bruises, no broken bones. No sign of injury at all. *Now what?*

I looked at the steep sides of the canal. *Could I climb out?* I doubted it. The muddy walls loomed at least eight feet high. *And how would I get my little nephew out?*

Then I thought about Marie. She could climb anything. I knew it would be a risk but I had no choice.

"Marie, do you think you could climb to the top?"

"Watch!" she dared. Without hesitation she scrambled up the muddy wall, finding footholds on rocks, bits of broken concrete, tufts of grass and roots that jutted out. Triumphantly she heaved herself over the top, turned and stared down at us.

"Climb, Keenan, climb." I cheered my little nephew on. As he grabbed at plants growing on the dirt wall, I shoved his padded bottom upward. "Marie, lie down and grab Keenan's hands. Good. Pull!" I coached. She yanked him up over the side. "Now sit down and hang on to him tightly."

Taking my cues from Marie's assent, I assaulted the slick wall. After losing my footing once, then twice, I finally joined the kids.

I looked down at the car sitting on the only flat surface at the bottom of the ravine. Every other area was covered with huge chunks of concrete. I marveled that we had escaped unharmed, and thanked God again.

We hiked to the nearest house. We knocked. No answer. We went on to the next. As we approached, the door flung open. I told the woman what had happened.

"Oh, sweetie, do come in," she said without hesitation. Before handing me the phone she said, "Can I ask you a personal question?"

"Yes," I said tentatively.

"Do you believe in God? I mean, do you know how many people have died at that same spot? Just six months ago, two teenagers drowned right there. It's just a miracle you all aren't hurt."

Later, the highway patrolman said, "I don't need to ask if those kids were strapped in, Ma'am." Then he added, "They'd be dead for sure if they weren't. It's a wonder you all weren't hurt. Do you believe in God?"

"Do you believe in God, lady?" the tow truck driver echoed as he ruefully considered how to hoist the car out of the canal.

The repairman at the station circled the car assessing the damage. "It's totaled, no doubt about it. You say no one was hurt?" I nodded and he continued. "It's a wonder. I don't know about you, but I believe God had a hand in keeping you and those little ones safe. Do you believe in God?"

"Why Mama, why?" Marie's question brought me back to the present and the gruesome picture. "Why weren't we hurt? Not one little bit?"

"I don't know, dear," I answered honestly. "But I do know that the God we believe in watches out for us."

She smiled. "I need more pictures, Mom. Mr. Martinez says . . ."

Lynn Dean

Sunset in the Rearview Mirror

*Destiny is not a matter of chance, it is a
matter of choice. It is not a thing to be waited
for, it is a thing to be achieved.*

WILLIAM JENNINGS BRYAN

It was almost dusk as I drove home from
work one night, the setting sun on my left.
With a slight headache, my thoughts drifted
through my day at work at the domestic violence shelter, where we never know from
one moment to the next what to expect.

As I drove I thought of my life and all the
changes that had come about. I, too, had
once been the victim of domestic violence. I
was never beaten. I was threatened, yelled at,
and had things thrown at me, but I never

identified this as abuse. I'd always thought abuse was hitting and physical pain.

The sky was slowly darkening, and the feathery wisps of clouds turned to pretty pastels as I drove along. I continued to keep one eye on the clouds as I watched the road and let my mind wander. I had often tried to reason with my husband. I would say he didn't need to yell—I could hear what he was trying to say. I just didn't always agree with him. Did we have to think the same way about everything? Was that what it meant to be submissive? I usually acquiesced. My husband was the head of the household; I was the wife. That was my role. Often I felt put down and betrayed—the butt of my husband's jokes. But my own husband wouldn't want to do that, would he? He loved me! I must be the cause of our problems. Soon, it became easier to just agree with my husband, rather than fight. I wanted peace at any cost. I didn't know the cost was giving up myself. And no one else seemed to notice—no one but me.

My life had begun with so much promise. I'd been a good student. I hadn't made many of the mistakes my classmates did. I thought

I was steady, reliable and a commonsense thinker. So why couldn't I do anything right in my marriage?

Thankfully, our three children were not the victims of my husband's violent temper—I was. And as long as that temper was directed at me, it didn't hurt my children, did it?

My car left the freeway, and I headed in the opposite direction of the beautiful sunset. I hated to leave the florescent sky behind, but my trip must continue. I was headed home.

Home, now, was not with that man. After sixteen years, I left him. Despite much counseling, I could find no way to reconcile our miserable marriage. When we sought the help of pastors and counselors, my husband always made it clear that I was the "bad guy." But by this time I was convinced that he didn't love me, and I realized how evil he had been.

My family was devastated by the divorce. No one in our family had ever divorced. It just wasn't done. My family's shame was almost worse than the bad marriage. There were secrets about my marriage that even they didn't know. I tried to explain, but I couldn't bring myself to relive the details.

They didn't trust me, so I was on my own. I learned to live with that pain as well, but I had never felt so lonely.

Seven years after the divorce, home was now an eighty-year-old farmhouse on a beautiful country road. I was remarried to a peaceful soul like myself, whom I learned I could trust. We worked together on our home—remodeling, landscaping, building. We were constructing more than a house— we were building a new life. My family was more understanding now, and my kids had weathered the rough years after the divorce, much as our farmhouse had weathered the winds of time. They were doing very well. "Staying together for the sake of the children," simply doesn't work—it's a lie. My children now know that everyone deserves respect, even mom.

I'd learned what marriage was really all about. As head of the household, a man was meant to lead, but not bully, push, manipulate, threaten and criticize. My current husband was a gentle shepherd, not a drill sergeant. He was someone who could be respected and honored—a man of character and commitment. Power and control meant nothing to this man. He was committed to "love as Christ loved the Church."

Not far from home, I climbed a hill and suddenly was stirred out of my reverie. A brilliant sunset, more brilliant than any I'd ever seen, radiated in the rearview mirror. The vibrant oranges and vivid pinks held me spellbound. I rounded a turn at the top of the hill and pulled to the side of the road. With tears streaming down my face, I witnessed God's awesome creativity at work. I also knew exactly what he was trying to tell me at that very moment. While I was going through those hard times, God knew what I didn't. He knew that one day I would look back and see his brilliant master plan. God didn't put me through the abuse, but he used it to create a masterpiece—one I couldn't see at the time, but only when I looked back on it. I'd weathered the storm, and God was right there with me all the time. I was never alone.

I sat for several moments, drinking in the beauty of the incredible sunset. I eased back on the road and rounded another bend. That sunset was with me all the way home in the rearview mirror—just as God had been.

Sheryl Simons

More Chicken Soup?

We enjoy hearing your reactions to the stories in *Chicken Soup for the Soul* books. Please let us know what your favorite stories were and how they affected you.

Many of the stories and poems you enjoy in *Chicken Soup for the Soul* books are submitted by readers like you who had read earlier *Chicken Soup for the Soul* selections.

We invite you to contribute a story to one of these future volumes.

Stories may be up to 1,200 words and must uplift or inspire. To obtain a copy of our submission guidelines and a listing of upcoming *Chicken Soup* books, please write, fax or check our Web sites.

Chicken Soup for the Soul
P.O. Box 30880
Santa Barbara, CA 93130
fax: 805-563-2945
Web site: *www.chickensoup.com*

Passing It On

Out of our commitment to tithing, both personally and organizationally, it has become our tradition to donate a portion of the net sales of *Chicken Soup for the Soul* books to charities related to the theme of the book. In addition, tens of thousands of copies of *Chicken Soup for the Soul* books have been given to men and women in prisons, halfway houses, hospitals, churches and other organizations that serve adults and teenagers in need.

Due to the miraculous personal and spiritual transformations that have occurred for many inmates as a result of reading Chicken Soup books while in prison, Jack and Mark—along with prison volunteer Tom Lagana—undertook the compilation of *Chicken Soup for the Prisoner's Soul.*

A portion of the net sales of the original edition of *Chicken Soup for the Christian Woman's Soul* funds distribution of copies of *Chicken Soup for the Prisoner's Soul*, as well as *Chicken Soup for the Christian Woman's Soul* books free to incarcerated women. It is our hope and dream that we can use this tool that God has given us to change the lives, one story at a time, of those who desperately need to change.

Who Is Jack Canfield?

Jack Canfield is one of America's leading experts in the development of human potential and personal effectiveness. He is both a dynamic, entertaining speaker and a highly sought-after trainer. Jack has a wonderful ability to inform and inspire audiences toward increased levels of self-esteem and peak performance.

In addition to the *Chicken Soup for the Soul* series, Jack has coauthored numerous books, including his most recent release, *The Success Principles, How to Get From Where You Are to Where You Want to Be* with Janet Switzer, *The Aladdin Factor* with Mark Victor Hansen, *100 Ways to Build Self-Concept in the Classroom* with Harold C. Wells, *Heart at Work* with Jacqueline Miller and *The Power of Focus* with Les Hewitt and Mark Victor Hansen. He is regularly seen on television shows such as *Good Morning America, 20/20* and *NBC Nightly News*. For further information about Jack's books, tapes and training programs, or to schedule him for a presentation, please contact:

Self-Esteem Seminars
P.O. Box 30880
Santa Barbara, CA 93130
phone: 805-563-2935 • fax: 805-563-2945
Web site: *www.chickensoup.com*

Who Is Mark Victor Hansen?

In the area of human potential, no one is better known and more respected than Mark Victor Hansen. For more than thirty years, Mark has focused solely on helping people from all walks of life reshape their personal vision of what's possible.

He is a sought-after keynote speaker, bestselling author and marketing maven. Mark is a prolific writer with many bestselling books such as *The One Minute Millionaire, The Power of Focus, The Aladdin Factor* and *Dare to Win,* in addition to the *Chicken Soup for the Soul* series. Mark has appeared on *Oprah, CNN* and *The Today Show,* and has been featured in *Time, U.S. News & World Report, USA Today, New York Times* and *Entrepreneur* and countless radio and newspaper interviews.

As a passionate philanthropist and humanitarian, he has been the recipient of numerous awards that honor his entrepreneurial spirit, philanthropic heart and business acumen for his extraordinary life achievements, which stand as a powerful example that the free enterprise system still offers opportunity to all.

Mark Victor Hansen & Associates, Inc.
P.O. Box 7665
Newport Beach, CA 92658
phone: 949-764-2640 • fax: 949-722-6912
Web site: *www.markvictorhansen.com*

Who Are the Coauthors?

Patty Aubery is the vice president of The Canfield Training Group and Self-Esteem Seminars, Inc. and president of Chicken Soup for the Soul Enterprises, Inc. She has been a guest on over 150 local and nationally syndicated radio shows.

Nancy Mitchell Autio joined Chicken Soup for the Soul Enterprises in 1994. Nancy and Patty have coauthored *Chicken Soup for the Surviving Soul, Chicken Soup for the Christian Soul* and *Chicken Soup for the Expectant Mother's Soul.* Nancy is also the coauthor of *Chicken Soup for the Nurse's Soul.* Contact Patty or Nancy at:

The Canfield Training Group
P.O. Box 30880, Santa Barbara, CA 93130,
Phone: 1-805-563-2935 Fax: 805-563-2945.

LeAnn Thieman is a nationally acclaimed professional speaker and author. Her book, *This Must Be My Brother,* details her daring adventure of helping to rescue 300 babies as Saigon was falling to the Communists. LeAnn is one of *Chicken Soup's* most prolific writers, and is also the coauthor of *Chicken Soup for the Nurse's Soul.*

LeAnn Thieman
6600 Thompson Drive, Fort Collins, CO 80526
Ph: 970-223-1574,
www.*LeAnn Thieman.com*
E-mail: *LeAnn@LeAnn Thieman.com*

Contributors

If you would like to contact any of the contributors for information about their writing or would like to invite them to speak in your community, look for their contact information included in their biography.

Candy Abbot is a speaker bible study leader, founder of Delmarva Christian Writers' Fellowship and author of *Fruit-Bearer*. She and her husband Drew are partners in Fruit-Bearer Publishing, a desktop publishing service for beginning writers. Candy can be reached at P.O. Box 777, Georgetown, DE 19947 or *dabbott@dmv.com*.

Lynn Dean is a Colorado writer and the mother of three children ages eleven, fourteen and sixteen. Lynn has written over 500 parenting articles that have appeared in more than 100 national and regional publications in thirty states. You can contact Lynn by writing to her at P.O. Box 146, Timnath, CO 80547.

Nancy Hird continues to practice her leadership abilities: producing church dramas, organizing pastors' breakfasts and teaching Sunday school. She also writes. Her articles have appeared in *Discipleship Journal, The Lookout* and *Moody Magazine*. Her books for children are *Marty's Monster* and *Jessica Jacobs Did What?* She can be reached at *hirdne@christcom.net*.

Darlene Lawson and her husband live on a farm in Atlantic Canada. She credits her writing ability to being in touch with the beauty of God's handiwork that surrounds their farm. Darlene enjoys gardening, walking, singing in the church choir and the farmhouse filled with family and friends. E-mail *antenna@nb.sypatico.ca*.

Patricia Lorenz is an art-of-living writer and speaker, the author of three books, over 400 articles; a contributor to ten

Chicken Soup for the Soul books; thirteen *Daily Guideposts* books; numerous anthologies; and an award-winning columnist for two newspapers. For speaking engagements phone (800) 437-7577 or e-mail *patricialorenz@juno.com.*

Caron Loveless is a wife and mother who knows to expect surprising encounters with God. Bestselling author and coauthor of nine inspirational books, she writes for magazines including *Today's Christian Woman* and speaks on radio and television, and at seminars and retreats. Caron is the author of *Honey They Shrunk My Hormones* and serves as creative director at Discovery Church in Orlando, Florida. Contact Caron at *www.caronloveless.com.*

Dawn Nowakoski, along with her best friend and husband, John, make their home in Indiana. They have been abundantly blessed with eight little people between the ages of four and fourteen, all of who teach them lessons daily and remind them of God's plan. You can reach Dawn at *eightsenuf@hotmail.com.*

Robin Lee Jansen Shope received her bachelor of science, with honors, from the University of Wisconsin in Whitewater in 1975. She teachers middle school in Lewisville, Texas. Robin enjoys reading, writing and working with children and young adults. Saturday mornings you will find her perusing flea markets or rummaging through local garage sales. Her dream is to have a novel published. She would enjoy hearing from you at *hi2Robin@attbi.com.*

W.W. Meade's extensive list of publishing credits includes *Cosmopolitan, Redbook* and the *Reader's Digest.* He has been a Managing Editor of the *Reader's Digest* Book Club and later of *Cosmopolitan.* Walker served as President and Editor in Chief of Avon Books for ten years before moving to Florida where he now resides.

Also Available

Chicken Soup African American Soul
Chicken Soup Body and Soul
Chicken Soup Bride's Soul
Chicken Soup Caregiver's Soul
Chicken Soup Cat and Dog Lover's Soul
Chicken Soup Christian Family Soul
Chicken Soup Christian Soul
Chicken Soup College Soul
Chicken Soup Country Soul
Chicken Soup Couple's Soul
Chicken Soup Expectant Mother's Soul
Chicken Soup Father's Soul
Chicken Soup Fisherman's Soul
Chicken Soup Girlfriend's Soul
Chicken Soup Golden Soul
Chicken Soup Golfer's Soul, Vol. I, II
Chicken Soup Horse Lover's Soul
Chicken Soup Inspire a Woman's Soul
Chicken Soup Kid's Soul
Chicken Soup Mother's Soul, Vol. I, II
Chicken Soup Nature Lover's Soul
Chicken Soup Parent's Soul
Chicken Soup Pet Lover's Soul
Chicken Soup Preteen Soul, Vol. I, II
Chicken Soup Single's Soul
Chicken Soup Soul, Vol. I-VI
Chicken Soup at Work
Chicken Soup Sports Fan's Soul
Chicken Soup Teenage Soul, Vol. I-IV
Chicken Soup Woman's Soul, Vol. I, II
